KANYE WEST

Gareth Stevens
Publishing

By Ethan Grucella

Please visit our website, www.garethstevens.com. For a free color catalog of all our high-quality books, call toll free 1-800-542-2595 or fax 1-877-542-2596.

Library of Congress Cataloging-in-Publication Data

Grucella, Ethan.
Kanye West / Ethan Grucella.
    p. cm. — (Hip-hop headliners)
Includes bibliographical references and index.
ISBN 978-1-4339-6614-9 (pbk.)
ISBN 978-1-4339-6615-6 (6-pack)
ISBN 978-1-4339-6612-5 (library binding)
1. West, Kanye—Juvenile literature. 2. Rap musicians—United States—Biography—Juvenile literature. I. Title.
ML3930.W42G78 2012
782.421649092—dc23

[B]

C. 1

                    2011027102

First Edition

Published in 2012 by
Gareth Stevens Publishing
111 East 14th Street, Suite 349
New York, NY 10003

Copyright © 2012 Gareth Stevens Publishing

Designer: Haley W. Harasymiw
Editor: Therese M. Shea

Photo credits: Cover background Shutterstock.com; cover, p. 1 (Kanye) Bruce Glikas/FilmMagic/Getty Images; p. 5 Frederick M. Brown/Getty Images; p. 7 Amanda Edwards/Getty Images; pp. 9, 11, 17, 19 Frank Micelotta/Getty Images; pp. 13, 25 Kevin Winter/Getty Images; p. 15 Matthew Peyton/Getty Images; p. 21 Larry Busacca/WireImage/Getty Images; p. 23 Brad Barket/Getty Images; p. 27 Leon Neal/Getty Images; p. 29 Mike Coppola/Getty Images.

Printed in the United States of America

CPSIA compliance information: Batch #CW12GS: For further information contact Gareth Stevens, New York, New York at 1-800-542-2595.

3/13

Contents

Talking Kanye

Kanye West always has people talking. He likes it that way! This hip-hop star is known for being outspoken.

Sweet Home Chicago

Kanye Omari West was born on June 8, 1977. His family lived in Atlanta, Georgia. When he was young, he moved to Chicago, Illinois.

Kanye spent most of his young life with his mother. She was a college teacher. She taught in China for a year. Kanye went with her.

Donda West

Kanye went to the same college where his mother taught. He wanted to break into the music business. He decided to move to New York.

Producing Hits

Kanye began as a music producer. He helped rappers Ludacris and Common make hit songs. Hip-hop superstar Jay-Z liked his work. He asked Kanye to work with him.

Common

13

Jay-Z's 2001 album was called *The Blueprint*. Kanye produced one of the biggest hits, "Izzo (H.O.V.A.)." For this song, Kanye mixed new and old music. People loved how it sounded.

Jay-Z

The Albums

Kanye decided to put out his own album. He worked hard. One night, he fell asleep while driving and crashed. Kanye wrote a song about this time. It was called "Through the Wire."

Finally, in 2004, Kanye's album came out. He called it *The College Dropout*. It sold over 400,000 copies in the first week!

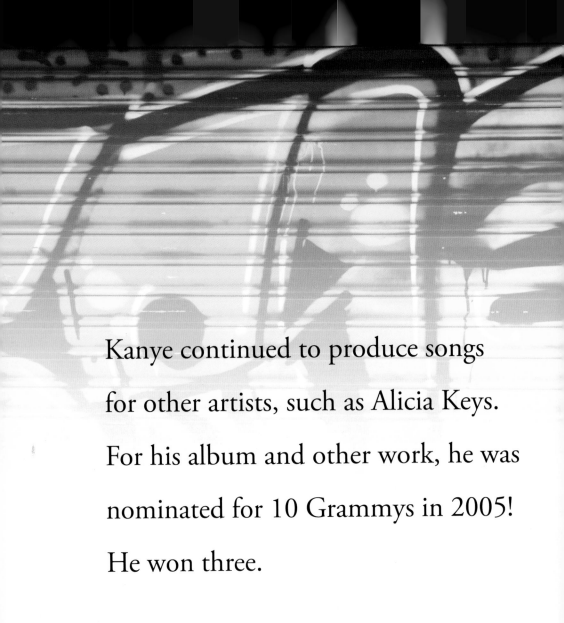

Kanye continued to produce songs for other artists, such as Alicia Keys. For his album and other work, he was nominated for 10 Grammys in 2005! He won three.

Alicia Keys

Chicago named February 27, 2005, "Kanye West Day"! That same year, he put out his second album. It was called *Late Registration*.

Kanye's second album reached number 1 on the music charts. It later won the Grammy for Album of the Year. Kanye kept writing. His next album, *Graduation*, won Rap Album of the Year.

25

In 2007, Kanye's mother died. He sang about his sadness on his 2008 album, *808s & Heartbreak*. He was back to rapping on his fifth album in 2010. It was another chart topper.

The One and Only

Kanye's name means "the only one." He says he wants to be number 1 in hip-hop music. Each number 1 album puts him that much closer.

Timeline

1977 Kanye Omari West is born in Atlanta, Georgia.

1996 Kanye goes to New York to break into the music business.

2001 Jay-Z and Kanye's album *The Blueprint* comes out.

2002 Kanye is in a car crash.

2004 Kanye's first album comes out.

2005 Kanye wins three Grammys.

2007 Kanye's mother dies.

2010 Kanye's fifth album hits number 1 on the charts.

For More Information

Books

La Bella, Laura. *Kanye West*. New York, NY: Rosen Publishing, 2009.

Sheen, Barbara. *Kanye West*. Detroit, MI: Lucent Books, 2010.

Weicker, Gretchen. *Kanye West: Hip-Hop Star*. Berkeley Heights, NJ: Enslow Publishers, 2009.

Websites

Kanye West

www.people.com/people/kanye_west/
Read fun facts about Kanye's life.

Kanye West Biography

www.biography.com/articles/Kanye-West-362922
Read more about Kanye's life and hit songs.

Glossary

college: a school after high school

Grammy: an honor given to someone for their music

nominate: to suggest someone for an honor

outspoken: speaking your mind without fear

producer: one who helps make a piece of music

Index